PHASES OF SANITY

Babble On

Magic and the magnitude of that magic can only be seen by those who love.

DEANNA CARR

authorHOUSE®

AuthorHouse™
1663 Liberty Drive
Bloomington, IN 47403
www.authorhouse.com
Phone: 1-800-839-8640

First published by AuthorHouse 6/27/2011

ISBN: 978-1-4634-0056-9 (e)
ISBN: 978-1-4634-0055-2 (sc)

Library of Congress Control Number: 2011908052

Printed in the United States of America

Table of Contents

Words

There comes a time in every man's life when he must die.
Be good to others, and you will reap the harvest of Peace.
Unkindness in your space will achieve you no Peace,
for those you leave behind will remember.
Live as you wish to die.
Though happiness may not surround you, your Peace will come.
In a place where there is no human sorrow,
your soul will rejoice in its freedom.

Love, After the Death of Love

I feel I am melting away from myself.
Am I looking for love by making love?
Or am I having sex to fill the void love has left?
Looking at the still perfection of the candle's flame,
I see the brilliant flame of Eternity in its virginity,
Purging the air of polluting impurities.
Can it rid me of my impurities?
Am I to be purged by fire?
Is this how I will die?

Untitled

From the still and battered carcass,
Of a love that was divine,
Can we find that sentiment
Where you can call me thine?

The Beach

Lonesome, I sit in silence,
In a world of icy millions;
Like a solitary pebble
On a cold and sandy beach,
Hoping that someday I might live
In a garden of loveliness.

In eons to come, the tides of time
May wear my edges down,
My Self will then be scattered
And my fibers, then, would blend
To match and to mingle with
All other grains of sand
In this world of icy millions,
For they also once were pebbles
Cast upon this barren land.

If I remain constant in my desire,
I could become a silent ember,
And, I with others like me
Could warm this troubled earth
Sharing the warmth within us
With the fragments of our fellow man
Making this beach a better place,
To cast our pebbles on.

If all that I imagine
Could come to be some day
Then I'd no longer sit alone
And, fearful, have to say
That I am all alone like you
On this, a brand new day.

But, what if the ice defeats me
And shakes my hope and warmth?
Would I become as they are?
Cold and hopeless too?
This cannot happen to me
I feel it in my soul
And I am consumed with passion
As I extend my Self
To You.

Glasses

Men don't make passes
At girls who wear glasses.
Now, we know, lads and lasses
That men do make passes
In masses and masses
At girls who wear glasses
While we, on our asses
Wait for the passes
The girls who wear glasses
Pass on!

Near to You

When you are near
I experience
A pleasurable palpitation
Surge through my breast
And I am warmed
By your radiance.

Give One's Self

It takes the death of one's Self
To know that The Self will never die
In the hearts of those you have given
A small part of your Self.

The Touch

The burning of your touch
Turns my soul to an inferno
That can only be quenched
By cascades of your kisses
Ending in passion of unmatched intensity
Then cooled by the tidal afterglow of ecstasy!

Backstabbers

Backstabbers are a funny breed,
As some of you may know,
A smiling face and friendly ways
Are the aims before the throw.

They'll talk to you in private
Of things, best left unsaid,
But should you slip just once you know
You may as well be dead.

They wait around like alley cats
Their prey upon to pounce,
And when the knife is finally stuck,
Its weight is pound for ounce.

Backstabbing is a special art,
It takes much time and thought,
To pick the ones who won't fight back,
One's name they'd never blot.

We've seen this creature many times,
In many shapes and forms.
A victim seldom ever knows,
They are different from the norm.

Minor Confession

I truly hate to say it,
But I really must confess
That when you are not near me
My life is such a mess.

I just don't understand it,
I'd surely like to know,
Why, when you are near me
My feelings never show.

It's not because I mean to
Be distant and aloof
Because, you see, I love you
And darling that's the truth.

Evening's Silence

Softly drifting through eventide
As time ticks slowly on,
Sweet silence whispers in my ear
The shadows will soon be gone.

To Be

Stone faced I stand
In icy silence,
Chiseled hard by natures hand,
Raw and jagged here
Where none can see
But the virgin sky of tomorrow.

Untouched by emotion
I exist in silence
My wait has been empty and long
For a master to come
And tenderly free
That which is captive
Inside of me.

Behold my shapeless mass
And gently carve this stone
Molding my craggy face
To create a thing of beauty
Which, when done,
My soul will be free to soar.

To be given to form
Has been my desire
For eons of endless time
By a masters touch
I would be free to feel
That which I pine for;
Love.

Waifs

Waifs are just like other kids
With childish joys and fears,
But, unlike lots of other kids
Must learn to hide their tears.

They know not what the morrow brings
As they trip from home to home
They dream of love, and other things,
Like not to be alone.

It's hard to call her mother,
They've said that word before,
They don't know one mom from another
It makes their small hearts sore.

Waifs must try to understand
A life they cannot bear,
And they hope that where they stand
There is love enough to spare.

They need the love of family life,
And to know their journey's ended,
To no longer feel the bitter strife,
Of a young life left … suspended.

Memories

Memories may fade by and by
But rendered in ink they'll never die.

Misses, Mr.'s, and Mrs.

Kisses are only kisses,
And Misses become Mrs.
But when Mr. misses Mrs.
Then Mrs. misses kisses.

One Reason I Write

I need your love and tender touch
And all things that go with them,
To say, "I love you very much"
Is why I write this poem.

I want to tell you how I feel
In a way you'll understand
Maybe, to you, it's no big deal
But, I love to hold your hand.

To join together hand in hand
Is such a lovely feeling
You know, to me, it's grand
And sets my heart to reeling.

Your kisses too, though pecks my be
Are none the less consuming,
When coupled with a squeeze you see
They start my love to blooming.

To lay with you at end of day
And hold your body close
Is just the funny way I say
"My darling, you're the most!"

Take Him

Have you ever chanced to meet him?
The God of Love incarnate,
In the frame of a man so tender
With fire as deep as garnet
He will take your love's sweet ember
And flame it to its summit.

Have faith, my trembling friend,
Your God of Love will come.
He'll steal your heart so sweetly,
Take your speech and leave you dumb,
Just take this man discreetly,
And bask in what he's done.

My World

My life is just so lovely now,
So comfortable and refined,
The thought of changing it at all,
Is furthest from my mind.

When we started out, it seemed,
Our union was unstable,
We tried to make it work, you know,
As hard as we were able.

Now we have a lovely home,
With many lovely things,
You your skis and sports cars
And me my shining rings.

We make a fair good living,
With money left to save,
And all that we have sacrificed,
Our friends say we were brave.

You hear me speak of our good life,
That's not what it's about,
Inside my heart, I want to cry,
"I'm trapped … God let me out!"

Help

Sometimes it seems so useless,
This struggle to survive,
It takes much time and patience,
Just to stay alive.

Everyone needs a helping hand,
Every now and then,
So stretch your hand out neighbor,
And guide your fellow man.

Letter To A Love

Each time that I am with you,
The fires of love abound,
But should I say, "I'm busy",
You don't want me around.

You say you love me; maybe,
Too soon, again, I'll add,
But when plans don't include you,
You become irrational and mad.

I just don't understand it,
Why when we're on the town,
You bring me home for payment,
You know that brings me down.

You know I care a lot dear
It's just too soon to say,
That maybe, in the future,
Together we might stay.

I've never met a person,
Who's meant so much so fast,
But give it time to grow dear,
And maybe we will last.

If I Were Rich

If I were filthy rich
I would be in such a stitch
And get me such an itch
That I wouldn't know just which
To give up being rich
Or sit and itch and twitch!

Birthday wish

So your birthday's come, at last,
Live it up, but not half-assed!

How Could You

I needed you,
But where were you,
You were by my side
But with someone new.

Refrain;
How could you
How could you do this to me?

I gave my all,
At your beck and call,
Now you've passed me by
For a painted doll.

In your silent mind,
You were so unkind,
In your sleep you spoke
Her name, not mine.

Refrain;
How could you
How could you do this to me?

Now you're all alone,
Just as cold as stone,
And you call to me,
But it chills my bone.

Should I take you back?
Take the love I lack,
Like I'm still your puppet,
Just pull up the slack.

Refrain;
How can I
How can I do this to me?

Freckles

Freckles, freckles
All over the place,
I get so embarrassed
I hide my face.

On my cheeks
And on my nose,
Across my brow
Down to my toes.

Some say they are wholesome!
Some say they're cute!
Others say charming
Or healthy, to boot!

I say it's not nice
This uneven tan,
When mentioned I blush
And shield with my hand.

Then somebody asked me,
"Do you know what this is?"
He said they are merely
A butterfly's kisses.

A butterfly came
With love and care
My face, like a blossom
Left nectar there.

The sun brings depth
From the nectar pools,
And their sweetness grows
Into beauty's tools.

Freckles, freckles,
All over the place,
I feel so proud
They adorn my face.

The Way I Feel

It's too soon to tell, but I think I do,
It seems I've come to fall for you.
It's not your looks, or even charms,
Could be the warmth within your arms.

The warmth I feel is truly grand,
It takes me to a love sweet land.
Wrapped in your arms, or by your side,
I'm swept into your loving tide.

Near or far, my thoughts and dreams,
Are all about your loving beams,
Your love's so warm it stokes my fire,
And make you, dear, my one desire.

Quench my thirst and fill my life,
That we shan't know of lover's strife.
You gave the spark of love's sweet flame,
From now, my life won't be the same.

Fulfill me now, as I will you,
Our love will be so bright and new,
Within our hearts the love will last
The future is now, it has no past.

Love's Captive Soul

Somewhere along life's twisted avenues,
Through the glittering beauty and degradation,
I must have done something right
To find myself in your tender embrace,
And to gaze into your eyes.

Pressing close against your strength,
I know the joy of being woman,
For I was born to love and satisfy
Him who captures my soul.

Not noticing when you captured me,
I succumbed to your manly way,
Now holding my love as a captive bird
Trembling, not longer in fear,
But with desire to be consumed by your essence.

Friends

Old friends, new friends,
Strangers passing by,
Lovers of the even' time,
Just flames to the eye.

Friends in love with music,
Some with god above,
Many loving people,
Some of whom you love.

Friends who stick by you
Whether you are right or wrong,
They are there to guide you,
With you all along.

Friends who need no reason
For the things they do,
When you've lost the very thing,
That you thought was you.

Friends are like the diamonds,
Sparkling clear and true,
And never say without one,
You could e'er be you.

Behold

Behold the work of God, my friend,
And shake within your pants,
If it weren't for Him, you know,
We might be ruled by ants!

Behold the work of God, my boy,
While gazing at the lasses,
If not for His ozone layer,
We'd be but seething masses!

Behold the work of God, my girl,
We could walk on all fours,
And then, my word, what would you do,
For opening the doors?

Behold the work of God, my dear,
As we lay enwrapped like this,
If not for the Sin of Eden,
We wouldn't know such bliss!

Behold the work of God, my friend,
And cater to his whims,
If crossed He could change 'hims to 'hers
Or change all 'hers to 'hims.

Wedding Toast

May you always be a joyous,
As this your wedding day.
May happiness surround you,
And always smile your way.

I know the vows you spoke today,
Will long live in your hearts,
So shed the old and don the new,
From here your new life starts.

I trust you'll live in harmony,
And share in love's array,
So always, be as happy,
As this, your wedding day.

Chain of Events

Let me take your trembling hand,
And hold it tight in mine,
So I can say the things I planned,
And see your bright eyes shine.

Please come to me and sit a while,
As I take some time to think,
And better, I'll see your lovely smile,
That thrills me to the brink.

Refrain:
You are everything to me
And oft' times so much more,
And as I hold you tenderly,
My love swells from my core.

Won't you please lay by my side?
As thunder fills my heart,
I wish you would with me abide,
And allow our love to start.

Refrain:
You are everything to me
And oft' times so much more,
And as I hold you tenderly,
My love swells from my core.

Thank you, babe, for everything,
It really has been fun,
You know, it's such a funny thing,
But I really have to run.

Refrain:
You were everything to me
But not so any more,
You let me take you easily,
I'm sure you know the score.

Thank you, babe, for everything,
It really has been fun,
You know, it's such a funny thing,
But I really have to run.

Our Time Has Come

Our time has come to say goodbyes,
Oh sweet darling please don't cry.
I told you many times before,
One day I'd walk out of your door.

You gave your love with open eyes,
No tears there'd be at our goodbye,
Before me now, you trembling, stand,
Desperate, clinging to my hand.

Refrain:
My life has only just begun,
I must go from sun to sun,
Today I'm only passing time,
With no reason, and no rhyme.

Release me now and set me free,
When I am gone, you'll surely see,
To follow me is not your need,
I need my freedom to succeed.

Forget me as I quit your side,
Best the pain you'll then abide,
Our love could never satisfy,
The part of me that needs to fly.

Refrain:
My life has only just begun,
I must go from sun to sun,
Today I'm only passing time,
With no reason, and no rhyme.

The light is dim and shadows grow,
My time, at last, has come to go,
This day, you knew, would come along,
When I must sing a brand new song.

Refrain:
My life has only just begun,
I must go from sun to sun,
Today I'm only passing time,
With no reason, and no rhyme.

She's Leaving

She told me she was leaving,
And not to worry none.
She said she never loved me,
But still she bore my son.

She's taking him away from me,
My world just fell apart,
She's leaving in the morning,
And packing up my heart.

Refrain:
How can she do this to me?
To make me feel this way,
To take away my little boy,
Who brightened every day?

As I sit here pondering,
The words she calmly spoke,
I think that on this whiskey,
I'm surely going to choke.

The bottle, here before me,
Brings back a memory,
Of when I'd hold our little boy,
And feed him upon my knee.

Refrain:
How can she do this to me?
To make me feel this way,
To take away my little boy,
Who brightened every day?

She's killing me, it's plain to see,
This whiskey tells me so,
She's taking all I ever had,
Plus dreams of long ago.

I often dreamed of things to come,
My son tall by my side,
Of how we'd be together,
Walking stride for stride.

Refrain:

It's time to leave this bar room,
The morning's creeping on,
Soon my wife and little boy,
From me will be gone.

Ice Breaker

If you want some loving,
Of the impassioned kind
Kindly call this number,
For that is what you'll find.

When Evening Comes

Come to me softly darling,
As twilight gently falls,
Tumbling down sweet shadows,
As dusky breezes call
To every lover, near and far.
Come hold me darling.

The flaming shades of evening,
Are burning in your eyes,
They touch your face with fire,
As we find our paradise
For we are lovers, here and now.
Come take me darling.

The crimson skies are fading,
To a vibrant purple hue,
As we bask in tidal afterglow,
Of a love that seems so new,
Yet we've been lovers for some time.
I love you darling.

Come to me softly darling,
As twilight gently falls,
Tumbling down sweet shadows,
As dusky breezes call
To every lover, near and far.
Come hold me darling.

Come Back To Me

I bought your love with tender lies
Of the warmth within my heart.
I told you how my heart took flight,
A lie, right from the start.

You found me out, and packed your things
And left me standing there,
You swore you'd not return to me,
But I didn't really care.

I waited for my phone to ring,
Or to greet you at my door,
But you, I fear, will never come,
It's been ten months and more.

Though I was lying at the time,
I cannot say that now,
I've fallen, hard, in love with you,
Of that, my sweet, I vow.

Please return to me once more,
And still the trembling in my heart,
I love you now, and that is true,
Though not so at the start.

Don't forsake me for the past,
I've learned about the pain,
Forgive me love, and please return
Let me love you now, again.

Please tell me, dear, that you still care,
And come back to my side,
Without you in my emptiness,
I simply can't survive.

Though I was lying at the time,
I cannot say that now,
I've fallen, hard, in love with you,
On that, my sweet, I vow.

Fading

The darkest day of my life,
Just happened yesterday,
I had to tell my only love
That I must go away;
My time is nearing.

It hurts me so to see him,
With sad and tear filled eyes,
He holds me close and kisses me
And even still, he cries,
For I am leaving.

You know that it's not easy,
These things I have to say,
So let us grasp each moment
And cherish each new day,
For I'm still living.

They tell me I am fading,
My life, it soon will end,
So now's the time, my darling,
I really need a friend,
They say I'm fading.

Please love me now as always,
Though time is running out,
I cannot say I'm unfulfilled,
For I know what love's about;
I don't fear dying.

Your love has made it easier,
I'll fight Fate to the end,
With you beside me I could win,
On Hope I will depend,
My hope you're giving.

Don't think about tomorrow,
It never really comes,
Because today I'm living,
We'll beat the victory drums,
For I'm still living.

My time to go is closing in,
I feel its grip on me,
Please hold me close and whisper,
This end just will not be.
We must keep fighting.

Time is racing forward,
My fight is almost done,
So let me lean upon you,
And tell me when we've won.
I can't be dying.

The time to go has passed me by,
My eyes are open wide,
I am here and still alive,
We've spurned Death's awful tide,
Yes I am living.

In jubilation I can shout,
Life's such a precious thing,
It seems so very bright and new,
Each morning makes me sing
Thank God, I am still living!"

The Door To Love

The door to love is open
It swings both to and fro,
But when you'll meet your own true love,
You will never know.

The path could be a rocky one,
Or smooth as silk can be,
Strewn with briars and brambles,
Or clear and trouble free.

Love is waiting everywhere,
Just hidden by that door,
So go and push it open,
To love for evermore.

The door to love is open,
It swings both to and fro,
But when you'll find your own true love,
You will never know.

Helping You

Whene'er life's little tragedies,
Seem much to hard to bear,
Remember I am at your side,
Your burden for to share.

Take my hand and lean on me,
For inner strength to find,
And never hold your feelings back,
Become part of my mind.

You know that I've been through it,
I can help to ease your pain,
So then, we two, can closer grow,
And taste sweet love again.

The first hurt is the hardest,
Of this, I'm sure you know,
But if two people share it,
The pain will quickly go.

Take my help and you will see,
That what I say is true,
Then confusion soon will pass,
And you'll know just what to do.

To help with disappointments,
Is what friends are all about,
To share the joys and sorrows,
Of this, there is no doubt.

I will stand beside you,
To share each landed blow,
To guide you through your darkness,
The way to light, I'll show.

Come let me, then, embrace you,
Whene'er you feel unsure,
I'll be your shelter in the storm.
Together, we'll endure.

Had To Say Goodbye

You know our life together,
Was less than paradise,
But something held me to you,
The bond was in your eyes.

Refrain:
Sometimes I am sorry,
For tossing you aside,
But now I find it easier,
To dry the tears I cried.

I was but a one-night stand,
And then just one night more,
That one-night stand became a month,
That month became a score.

We both knew it was futile,
To think of us as one.
And yet we both pursued it,
Like shade within the sun.

Refrain:
Sometimes I am sorry,
For tossing you aside,
But now I find it easier,
To dry the tears I cried.

I had to say farewell, my love,
But should we meet someday,
I hope that you won't hate me,
For leaving you this way.

You know our life together,
Was less than paradise,
But something held me to you,
The bond was in your eyes.

After The Leaving

I say that I am happy,
That we have parted ways,
But now I freedom,
I pass such lonely days.

It's not that I am all alone,
Because that's not the case,
It's simply that I feel alone,
In every crowded place.

No one sees the side of me,
I find I have to hide,
They never see the emptiness,
That now I feel inside.

It's hard for me to fathom why,
I feel so insecure,
I guess it's simply just because,
love's lost its sweet allure.

I don't regret our parting ways,
We knew it had to be,
Because there wasn't anything,
On which we could agree.

Some day it may happen,
Alone no more I'll be,
And I'll no longer feel my heart,
Is drifting out to sea.

Your Eyes

Your eyes are dark as the midnight sky,
As soft as velvety night,
That blankets the silent desert sands,
With the depth of eternal sight.

They speak with sensuous silence,
No need to vocalize,
And I am engulfed in their mystery,
When I gaze into your eyes.

Our Time

Our time has come,
Our time has gone,
And now it's time,
To travel on.

You came to me on wings of night,
When I was young and love was right,
We said our piece we sang our song,
How could we know it would go so wrong?

That it is done, there is no doubt,
So what is it I cry about?
There was no reason and no rhyme,
I guess we just ran out of time.

Our time has come,
Our time has gone,
And now it's time,
To travel on.

Wild Seed

Soaring lightly like a wild seed,
Tossed by the autumn breeze,
Searching for that sweet encounter,
That every young lover needs.

He came to me on a winter's eve,
And lovingly stayed through spring,
So warmly did I treat him,
His heart did sweetly sing.

He stayed through the warmth of summer,
Growing each day in splendor,
Thriving on love's sweet promise,
Of a bloom that could be so tender.

Autumn came, as petals did fall,
And the fruit of us was there,
The seeds were once again scattered,
With the ability to care.

Soaring lightly like a wild seed,
Tossed by the autumn breeze,
Searching for that sweet encounter,
That every young lover needs.

Reflections on Dining

Cracks upon a stucco wall,
Grease adorned and grey,
Is something I encounter,
Almost everyday.

The best of places pass me by,
A solo I do traipse,
To dine on coke and hamburgers,
While others dine on crepes.

There's something in the way I live,
That simply won't allow,
Caviar to pass my lips,
Just ground from fatted cow.

The atmosphere of candlelight,
Is what I long to know,
But all I get is jukebox jive,
And neon all aglow.

Leather clad upholstery,
And cozy dim lit booths,
Would better be than vinyl cracked,
And handy, raucous youths.

If I were one of those who could,
Take without a thought,
Then all that I could ever want,
For me, soon, would be bought.

So why do I continue,
To spurn their offers so?
I guess, within myself, I can't,
Allow my Self to go.

So I will just continue,
To eat in diners dim,
And munch on greasy hamburgers,
In hopes of meeting "HIM"

Closet Love

Whenever we should chance to meet,
You never seem to know me,
But when you want some loving,
You seem to think you own me.

You want me just to sit around,
And be your closet love,
But should I try to find someone,
You curse the stars above.

Why do you always come to me?
When ever you want sex,
Which you could get from anyone,
My mind, it does perplex.

A closet love is not my need,
I wish ours could be real,
But then again, you never think,
Of the way that I might feel.

You love me only when it seems,
That it would serve you best,
You never allow me to be me,
Please give my heart a rest.

You've torn my heart asunder,
You took the best I had,
To know that I still love you,
Should make your heart feel glad.

We split so many moons ago,
Now you've a woman new,
But still you want me on the side,
While all I want is you.

Waiting

Our beings met, but once in time,
I've lacked your presence since,
I'm waiting now, in silence,
For the entrance of my prince.

Dreams have found us riding,
Through sultry steaming forests,
By placid lakes and racing streams,
An experience that love made for us.

You entered in on silent wings,
And soft, your presence stays,
The joy you've brought into my life,
Will last through many days.

Waiting now, to meet again,
A flash comes to my eye,
For there you stand, across the room,
Again my heart does fly.

Misplaced Aloneness

Have you ever stopped to wonder,
As in solitude you sit,
Why you are so all alone,
In crowds, you just don't fit?

Could it be that what you feel,
Is not the thing you show?
Or could it be you can't relate,
But want them all to know?

You see them all as cold as ice,
So distant, so unyielding,
But could it be that they see you,
As cold, and thus unfeeling?

Take your foolish human pride,
And swallow it down whole,
Take that step to break the ice,
And cheer two lonely souls.

To You

I've met a lot of people,
I guess I've been around,
But someone who,
Is sweet as you,
Never have I found.

I've not been many places,
Though I hope that I just might,
Stay where I've been,
At the place I've seen,
In your eyes, by firelight.

Voices

Voices calling in the lonely night,
You run blindly toward the sound,
Desperate, you seek the unseen promise,
And weep, for it cannot be found.

The thunder beating in your breast,
Does shake the heavens above,
Drowning out the voices,
That calls to you for love.

Reflection

There is always someone,
To whom you owe your misery,
Look carefully as you find,
The enemy in your own reflection.

Wisdoms Draught

Drink wisely from the well of experience,
And reap the eternal reward of knowledge.

Quest

Running and searching,
Leaving the living,
Wanting to be needed,
Needing to be giving.

Desperate is each step,
And, urgent, every glance,
Giving yourself to everyone,
Hoping Love will take a chance.

What You Are

My darling let me tell you,
Just what you mean to me,
You are my starlight of the evening,
Reflected in the sea.

You are the gentle summer breeze,
And the throbbing in my breast,
The crimson flames of sunset,
When we lay us down to rest.

You are my sunshine every morning,
You are my moonbeam every night,
The sweet song of the sparrow,
And butterflies in flight.

You are the love that is in my eyes,
And the fire within my heart,
Passions never ending flame,
That says we'll never part.

You are the sweetly scented roses,
Gently kissed by morning dew,
These things are what I think of,
When my thoughts come 'round to you.

Take Time

Take the time to see those around you,
For tomorrow, sight may be gone.

Thoughts

Thoughts are forming in my mind,
I cannot tell you why,
My heart is feeling tender things,
Ever since, you caught my eye.

Thoughts of loving, possible,
Of desires burning flame,
Things I've never thought of,
'til to my world you came.

Tenderness of the flaming kind,
Softly gentle, loving firm,
Make my body quiver,
With loves eternal term.

Summer Love

The lonely cry of the cicada,
Splits the sultry summers heat,
And hints of loves encounter,
That soon you'll chance to meet.

In the heat of the summers day,
Love shows its tender light,
Exploding in flaming passion,
In the silence of the night.

Don't Ask

Don't press on me
Your need to be
Loved, and shown compassion,
For don't you know it,
That if you show it,
It will come in its own ration.

Loves Demise

Seeing the emptiness in your eyes,
I feel the pain within your sighs,
Too long, you've listened to the lies,
How agonizing, Loves demise.

Under Cover Lonesome

I am, oh so lonely,
In the midst of all my lovers,
For they will never know me,
When I'm out from under covers.

They know not who I am,
Or who I'd chance to be,
I've something under covers,
That they will never see.

I am a woman, gendered,
Not unlike all the others,
So why is it I only find,
My solace under covers?

I need someone to help me,
Someone to be my friend,
A person I can lean on,
On whom I can depend.

I need the love of someone,
Who takes me as I am,
Someone who will love me,
Not making love a sham.

I wish someone would take me
And love me as no others,
So I'd no longer simply be,
Just someone under covers.

For I am, oh so lonely,
In the midst of all my lovers,
And they will never know me,
'til I'm out from under covers.

Ice Breaker 1

I've seen you from a distance,
Your beauty is beyond compare,
I'd like to get to know you,
If you think, I dare.

Returning From Death (By Natural Causes)

You lift gently from your mortal trappings,
Made of flesh and bone,
Drifting away from the self that was you,
Detached, unmoving … alone.

Watching, silently aware, yet unfeeling,
Your earthly self lay dormant,
The part of you that you now know,
Freed from mortal pain and torment

You miss the fleshy garb you wore,
But you know there is no need,
As you turn toward the blinding light,
Travelling swiftly, without speed.

Entering the corridor of blazing coolness,
The light is soothing, blue as Delft,
You are a vapor, not escaping,
But vaporizing unto yourself.

Travelling, with calm as your companion,
And awareness as your friend,
With the knowledge of all you'd sought,
In your life, now at an end.

Serene in believing you will be reborn,
Retaining your compassion and love,
You have no regret at your earthly time,
As you approach the light above.

A sense of wonder and contentment,
As a vision will materialize
A vision with question posed,
Shall you change this life of lies?

Suddenly, your vehicle of light turns,
You begin to plummet back to mortality,
Gaining speed for the entering,
Then, all is black and void of reality.

Your eyes open, and your head spins,
What was known, is somehow gone,
But a chance to create a better life,
You rejoice in Life's new dawn.

Travelers of Time

Across the room is where you meet,
Your eyes are the travelers of time,
They touch the space with silence
Flashing your minds sweet embrace

You speak without words or sound,
You know you soon will part,
Knowing you've touched a stranger
Who will long stay in your heart.

The only contact ever made,
Was between four messengers,
The windows of the heart and soul,
Your eyes, the travelers of time.

They bridge the gap the room has made,
They touch with sensuous silence,
They say that we have met today
Farewell and love be with you.

Loving

Loving is a giving thing,
When you give of yourself,
Love, and let your heart open,
To experience of the universe.

Openness will bring fulfillment.
As love enters into your heart,
First, you must open to the world,
Giving Love an open door,

Giving of yourself to someone,'
Will lead to a reward of excellence,
The excellence of knowing
That love is blooming universal

Take time to see around you,
Reach out your heart and hand,
Allow yourself to open up
Give love a fighting chance.

The Habit

It's a place of unlimited space,
Closing slowly to nothing,
Constricting the soul with torment,
Betraying the minds perception.

It chokes the breath from the body,
Leaving you gasping for reality,
You know not the real from fantasy,
As you race to nowhere, in confusion.

Did you see it? Or was it fiction?
You cannot feel that which is there,
Yet you feel that which is not,
And your mind hungers for an answer.

Hungering, you cannot take nourishment,
Thirsting, you cannot be quenched,
Needing, you hear not the offers,
Wanting, you cannot see it there.

Your sensitivity is lost in a maze,
Feeling desperately the death occurring,
Shaking in your body's addiction,
To the curse of the minds expansion.

Desperate, you try to overcome it,
Your body quakes at the emptiness,
You run blindly without direction,
Searching for your lost identity.

Cringing from the brutal awakening,
Shivering in naked vulnerability,
Searching for a hand to guide you,
Needing guidance from within.

You stand alone in silent panic,
Attempting to grasp your sanity,
Quivering in your secret jungle,
Hoping no one sees your disease.

You search for some spark of life,
But, your heart is an empty tomb,
The mind you once possessed,
Has been destroyed by your ignorance.

Morning

The gentle mist that rises,
Off the cold and steaming water,
Ushers in the morning,
To awaken Natures daughter.

Man Mountain

A giant of a man is he,
So tall, so strong his fire,
A heart as soft as velvet is,
A true voice of desire.

Statuesque he stands in splendor,
Free and sensuous in the breeze,
Loving, open and tender,
Eyes raging like summer seas.

His warmth, it is consuming,
His strength, is oh so tender,
His touch does have the power,
To make the heart surrender.

He speaks with tender rumblings,
Of tumultuous love inside,
Passion in every movement,
Ebbing loves sweet tide.

When he walks beside me,
Diminutive I seem,
But no one ever knows the height,
This man has lifted me.

A mountain of a man is he,
So tall, so strong his fire,
A heart as soft as velvet is,
A true voice of desire.

Weekend

The time of our arrival,
Was filled with sultry heat,
And lighted by the mystery,
Of the ghostly "Witches Moon".

The stars were the eyes of eternity,
Seeing us in our sensuality,
In our openness and loving,
Naked, we were part of the evening.

The morning broke, as always,
With the beauty of something new,
Of a love that was beginning
Of friendships that were forming.

Laughing gaily in the noontime,
We shared in the frolic of children,
Allowing the sun to caress us,
And bathe our souls with joy.

We took the day and explored it,
On the waterways of our loving,
It flowed so bright and sparkling,
As the sun flashes off the sea.

We all did love and enjoy,
All that was set before us,
Gazing upon the luscious feast,
Displayed by our own true mother.

We partook of the banquet of nature,
Enjoying the tenderness of us,
That is seldom seen, but hidden,
In the silence of our minds.

We plunged in with our reality,
Stripped of social inhibitions,
Exhilarated by the freedom,
That we had given each other.

We found a treasure in the stream,
And were awed by its beauty,
As we encountered others there
Also captured by Natures beckoning.

Travelling back to our Eden,
We filled the night with laughter,
As we spent the evening tenderly,
Entering the hearts of each other.

We loved and did happily play,
In the sunshine of the morning,
We shared a part of each other,
That seldom sees the light.

We slaked our thirst in the morning,
The sparkling wine of kings,
That which brings warmth to the body,
And a glow in the depths of the soul.

As we took our sustenance,
From the tender fruits of love,
We shared its sweet tart succulence,
But were sated by our new friendship.

We looked again upon our treasure,
Rendered from the stream,
Knowing that our stately prize,
Would be more precious in our minds.

Leaving what began with the "Witches Moon"
We reveled in its mystery.
Knowing it will never be,
Like the driftwood, left behind.

It will never be forgotten,
For each time that we meet,
We will, again, remember
The passion of our hearts true offering.

We came to this place, unknowing,
Of the love that we could find,
Together we came and were captured,
By the tender embrace of nature.

Seeing the last light of our weekend,
Was a lonely and lost encounter,
We knew revelry was ending,
But our hearts would always remember.

The Promise of Rain

The stormy heavens, rumbling,
Grey shades of purple hue,
Summon the Gods of thunder,
Breathing soft, steaming cool.

The trees, like blackened needles,
Pierce the brooding cloud,
Splitting the heavens anger,
Defying the thunders shroud.

Calm, we traverse the waters,
Praying for reprieve,
Hoping for safe landing,
Wishing to never leave.

Visions seen in shadows,
Pine, in bodies full,
Birch in lacy silhouette,
To the heart, a spectacle.

The sunset blazes white,
Streaming through clouds, broken,
Kissing the waters surface,
With a vow yet left unspoken.

The dark and mysterious sentinels,
That guards the forest floor,
Beseech the heavens teardrops,
To quench their thirst once more.

We feel the heavens tremble,
And see its flashing pride,
As the earth is bathed in teardrops,
That the sultry heavens cry.

Beginnings

To start a new relationship,
Just let yourself be real,
And let the ever loving world,
Know just how you feel.

But Once a Year

Emerging only once a year,
To the world, my self I show,
I come to take some souls away,
But little do they know.

All the while, I joke about,
The fact that I'm the devil,
Beguiling everyone I meet,
To come to Satan's level.

All year I burn to be released,
To harvest the crop of souls,
And take them to the depths of Hell,
To the furnace of burning coals.

Little do the people know,
About my mystery,
A subtle secret spell I spin,
Glittered webs of fantasy.

They call me "Little Devil',
It is music to my ears,
All year I play "Miss Good Heart'"
Accept, but once a year.

Question of Knowing

How can you say you know me?
When I know not myself,
I've always kept Me hidden,
Somewhere upon some shelf.

It's been so long since I have been,
I know not who I be,
But every time I talk to you,
More of my Self I see.

You're Getting Misty

Why are you getting misty?
Just thinking about
Your empty life,
And writing about your
Bitter strife,
While wanting to be
A loving wife,
You get so misty.

Oh, please stop getting misty.
Start thinking about
A better life,
Stop writing about
Your bitter strife,
I am asking you
To be my wife,
Now don't get misty.

Misty Lady Love Me

Refrain:
Oh misty lady, lovely lady,
Look at me, and love me maybe,
Misty lady, lovely lady,
Come to me and love me, crazy.

You've come so far and seen so much,
But you've never known a lovers touch.
Somehow, love has passed you by
And no one see you when you cry.

Refrain:
Oh misty lady, lovely lady,
Look at me, and love me maybe,
Misty lady, lovely lady,
Come to me and love me, crazy.

Loving me would not be bad,
For I would never make you sad,
Come let me wipe away your tears,
And I will help to calm your fears.

Please tear it down, this wall of stone,
Then you'd no longer be alone,
I love you now, and for all time,
I'm asking you to please be mine.

Refrain:
Oh misty lady, lovely lady,
Look at me, and love me maybe,
Misty lady, lovely lady,
Come to me and love me, crazy.

You've come so far, and seen so much,
But you've never known a lovers touch,
Please don't pass my loving by,
I'll be your comfort should you cry.

Refrain:
Oh misty lady, lovely lady,
Look at me, and love me maybe,
Misty lady, lovely lady,
Come to me and love me, crazy.

I'll Be Your Lady For a While.

Refrain:
I'll be your lady for a while,
I'll be your woman for today,
Take this love that I am giving,
Never make me go away.

Don't put up any fences,
Don't put reins on me,
The loving time we're sharing,
Must be based on honesty.

Refrain:
There may come a time to pass,
When I must go on my way,
Please don't hold me at my leaving,
For darling, this I'll say.

Refrain:
How long together we will stay,
Is something I cannot tell,
When my heart feels strain in staying,
Is when I'll say farewell.

Let us stay in love forever,
With freedom of the night,
For to you my heart is faithful,
While it's free as birds in flight.

Refrain:
Take this love I offer now,
Let us share our lives complete,
But never ask me for to wed
It would pain me to retreat.

Refrain:

The Chandelier

Here hangs the sparkling chandelier,
That bright the entrance makes,
Crying crystal teardrops,
In the emptiness of the hall.

It once rejoiced with laughter,
Of many beautiful people,
Who gazed upon its light,
And basked within its radiance.

Now, in the lonely foyer,
This lovely creation hangs,
Weeping at the loss of light,
Lonely tears of icy torment.

A lovely thing to be beheld,
In all its shimmering glory,
Dingy now, from much neglect.
No longer proudly glimmering.

Related Words

Words that kindle emotion,
Through darkness and despair,
Are never quite so keenly felt,
Than by those who have been there.

A Vision

A vision seen through silken veils,
Of tears that gently fall,
Inside the glass
Of a noon repast,
As memory pays a call.

To Late The Asking

Please don't take away my lips,
For I could not sing your praise,
Please don't take away my eyes,
For I could not see your beauty,
Please don't take away my ears
For I could not hear your wisdom,
Please don't take away my heart,
For I could not feel it pounding.

You have taken away my lips,
And set them aflame with passion,
You have taken away my eyes,
As I witness your enchantment,
You have taken away my ears,
So I can hear your naked truth,
You have taken away my heart,
And its thunder has consumed me.

Birthday Greeting

Birthdays will come,
And birthdays will go,
Some come too fast,
While others, too slow.

With whatever speed,
Its arrival this year,
I hope yours is happy,
And loaded with cheer.

I'm hoping the joy,
You're feeling today,
Will continue year long
Through every new day.

She In Springtime

She lifts her sleepy head,
And sheds the sleep of winter,
She feels the sun caress her,
Sensing life surge in her breast.

A long time has she slept,
Oblivious to passing bustle,
But now she is newly conscious
Of the miracle of new birth.

The sun is her own true lover,
As he kisses her, oh so warmly,
And she swells with the tender love,
He has bestowed upon her.

She is visited by many friends,
Some singing to her beauty,
Others keeping her company,
As she nestles them to her breast.

She cushions the path for any,
Who come to witness her birthing,
And she scents the air for those,
Who wish to keep her company.

She paints such lovely pictures,
With all colors of the rainbow,
And the heavens weep tears of joy,
Which she takes to nurse her infants.

The air is filled with a symphony,
Of songs sung to her glory,
And the chatter of those who need her,
And the sighs of those who want her.

She is a beauty to be beheld,
Newborn every spring,
So come and make her acquaintance,
Each time that she awakens.

Take her to your bosom,
And love her, as yourself,
For we are all part of her,
And she, is Mother Earth.

Flaming Sails

Coursing silently over sparkling sea,
The wind caressing our faces,
The sunset pierces the heavens blue
Flaming glory of evening traces.

Wrapped in the embrace of the night,
We race with hearts contentment,
Sailing on the seas of eternity,
And losing ourselves to enchantment.

The setting sun does torch the sea,
Blazing the horizon with fire,'
Freeing our hearts to fly,
On flaming wings of desire.

Of Johnny T

A stranger came unto me,
Through words not quite his own,
And since, we've been together,
For me a love has grown.

He's come to mean so very much,
In the short time we have been,
Still he has given something,
That he has not yet seen.

His absence, now, has just begun,
I feel it press on me,
Just how long must I live
With this love, he will not see.

Lonesome

When you are so lonely,
And no one seems to care,
When you really need them
They simply are not there.

You want and need somebody,
To say, "How do you do?"
But it just doesn't happen,
They never notice you.

You know that you are not alone,
We all get this disease,
But lonesome isn't terminal,
Its cure is such a breeze.

Take a look around you,
And see this dreaded thing,
The cure is there within you
To make a heart to sing.

Just smile at your neighbor
Or lend a helping hand,
Say hello to someone,
And find the feeling grand!

Your Gift

The warmth of your embrace
Gently holds my being,
As in the arms of the tropical sun.

The tenderness of your caress
Softly touches my soul,
Like the flutter of butterfly wings.

The burning of your kiss,
Sets my heart on fire,
With raging flames of sweet hot passion.

The loving countenance of you,
Has become my world,
And you have become my beloved.

Rape

Eyes, silent and cold as death,
Yet burning with violent purpose,
A body spurred on by desire,
To be quenched in raping violence.

Out of space, from another plane,
Unlimited power, endless time,
Unknown to the owner of the body,
To be succored by the incubus.

Sexual malice and violence,
It's only tempered release,
Is all the captive body feels,
But to the mind, all is lost.

He entered my room unnoticed,
During passion with another man,
Seeing, hearing and smelling,
Became enraged with carnal lust.

He waited until all was done,
And I, in my afterglow,
It had to shatter and disintegrate,
The beauty of my lover's balm.

It thrust himself upon me,
In conscience, unaware,
He became the incubus monster,
Violent lust it's only quest.

Loves Intensity

The intensity of the fire,
That burns within my heart
All but consumes me
With the magic of your art.

You came to me on silver wings,
As my lover and my friend,
When all my love was gone,
My emptiness to end.

Loves Gain Lost

Though much is gained
And much is lost,
By words that may be said,
There's nothing much
That can be done
To heal a heart that's dead.

Loves Bloom

I was yet a young bud blooming,
Still wrapped in infancy's gown,
Waiting to release the tender petals,
That have burst forth with your warmth,
Becoming the blushing bloom of love.
I have come to full flower of life,
To bloom forever in your light,
Tasting your loves sweet nectar,
And to kiss your face with pride.

Haunted Heart

My heart was like a haunted house,
Locked up against the world,
Clogged with mold
And cob webs old,
Where broken dreams were hurled.

Decrepit was that crumbling shell,
That once was filled with life,
With window veiled,
And beauty paled,
It stood in tortured strife.

The fading ember on the hearth,
Burned with silent longing,
To feel again
The tender flames
Of the heart, again, belonging.

You stood before this haunted place,
Which stirred the heart within,
Then in you came,
To fan the flame,
And allowed love to begin.

With care, you stoked the lonely hearth,
To awake with new desire,
Now all I see
Is the heart of me
Aflame with loves sweet fire.

Whirlwind

Caught in the whirlwind of your love,
And the flame of your desire,
I spiral uncontrollably,
On the wings of loves sweet fire.

Intangibles

Missing you, is the passing of time
'til I see you again.
Wanting you, is the flame of love
That burns so deep within.
Holding you, is the sweet reward
My soul has craved so long.
Loving you, is the deep desire
That bursts my heart with song.

Between the Lines

Read between the lines I write,
Or the words I may impart,
For then, you see,
My words could be
Heard within your heart.

If It Should Ever Happen

If it should ever happen,
That we might ever part,
There would be
A death in me
To long dwell in my heart.

Guarded Windows

Those ever guarded windows,
That opens to your heart,
Carefully hide
The need inside
You dare not to impart.

Loves Rosy Bloom

With the agony of losing,
And the pain of constant grooming,
We trim the rose
That ever grows
With love, forever blooming.

Fading Bloom

What happened to
The tender bloom
Of love, we thought so rare?
It withered stands
With drooping head
In want of loving care.

Your tender touch
And loving words
Could bring it back to life,
So take my hand
And touch my soul
To end this lovers strife.

Tug of Love

Two different worlds
Vying for control,
The battered battlefield
Is the third worlds soul.

One rival holds on,
The other, seducing,
Neither one winning,
Both of them losing.

The bond is so strong,
It's alive, yet dying,
But love for both worlds,
Leaves the wasted soul crying.

How long will it last?
Oh when will it end?
How long must I bleed,
Before this battlefield mends?

Lock and Key

I am the lock,
You are the key
So unlock my heart
And set me free.

Don't stop to wonder,
Never ask why
Our hearts take flight
To kiss the sky.

Troubled Love

The searing pain, that burns within,
Just grows with each new day,
The love we shared
Now seems impaired
And I feel it slip away.

You have become my everything,
My heart and souls desire,
What can I say
To make you stay
And fan this dying fire?

You're master of that throbbing drum,
Which beats beneath my breast,
Without you I
Would surely die
And lay me, sad, to rest.

Please help to ease this pain I bear,
And calm my troubled soul,
Let's be again
As we were then
For, dear, I love you so.

I Am

I am not the means
I am the end.
I am not the ticket,
I am the prize.
I am me
I am part of you

No Words

I have no words to tell,
Of the sadness in my heart,
Ever since, I realized,
That we two would part.

It's over, sounds so final,
Let's try to forget, won't do,
I'm leaving, shatters many dreams,
I'm sorry, is all too true.

Let us stay and love a while,
And hold each other tight,
Maybe love will start again,
With the coming of the light.

If the dawn shines brightly,
With the love between us two,
Then starting now, we'll ever grow,
In love forever new.

But if the dawn's still cloudy,
Then we can say we tried,
And I'll mark it on my calendar,
To proclaim the day I died.

Roberts Song

I have a need in me,
A need I thought no one could fill,
No one ever tried to see,
The tenderness that's with me still.

I have a love in me,
That cries out to find a home,
A love that promises ecstasy,
A love, when found, will never roam.

You came to me with your charms
You lifted me so high,
Within the circle of your arms,
I felt the fire in your eyes.

You found the need in me,
You lifted me to distant stars,
All along, you needed me,
How confused we lovers are.

I felt a need in me,
A need you have fulfilled,
You gave my life a harmony,
My trembling you have stilled.

Take this love in me,
Still the sobs and dry my tears,
Let me love you, and then you'll see,
Just like you, I'll calm your fears.

Souls Faces

Peoples faces looking sad,
Don't you wish to make them glad?
People stare with malice intent,
Can't they tell the soul is spent?

Can the heart that beats within,
Still the tempest born of sin?
Can the tender flames of love,
Lift the soul to stars above?

Look within the heart that dwells,
Within the chamber of human cells,
To find the fire that burns the soul,
And whispers low of loves untold.

Love Lost

How can I express the pain,
That burns so deep within?
How can a love so tender,
Allow hate to begin?

In the darkness surrounding me,
In my emptiness and pain,
I lay within my lonely bed,
And reach for you again.

Cold now, the flames of love,
Lost to a jealous heart,
How could love so beautiful,
So quickly, fall apart?

We did have a love so rare,
It put my soul to flight,
But now you say it's over,
My heart, now black as night.

I feel a burning emptiness,
A void within my heart,
You have taken away the sun,
To leave me in the dark.

I Thought You Hurt

I thought that once you left me,
The pain would be so great,
But now I see it isn't so,
Your leaving came too late.

It seems, while being with you,
The pain was greater still,
So now, I only feel relief,
And my heartaches now are still.

It's true you left me lonely,
With my faith a little marred,
But you didn't leave me empty,
Just sad and battle scarred.

It took the strain of trying,
To tell how much it pained,
To find I wasn't hurting,
And just how much I've gained.

I'll not again be overcome,
By the kind of man you are,
For now, I've found safe harbor,
Deep within my heart.

How Dare We Care

Sometimes I want to shout it,
And scream, I love you so,
But something always stops me,
When I feel that you may go.

How could we let it happen?
To let our feelings show,
We know you have no freedom,
For she'll never let you go.

Even still, when we are one,
In tender loves embrace,
Nothing in the world is wrong,
But the wrong we can't erase.

I know that when you leave me,
You'll be going home to her,
Leaving something else behind,
A pain that has no cure.

We have to stop this silly game,
It's foolish to pretend,
That we could be together,
But dare we let it end?

Two Parts of My Heart

I saw the envy in their eyes,
As we walked into the place,
Wishing they were in your shoes,
You could see it in each face.

They think that we are lovers,
Though we know, it isn't true,
But still we love each other,
As the rose loves morning dew.

I love you now, as always,
Though they will never know,
That we are just the greatest fans,
Of the best two folks we know.

Thank you, love, from me to you,
Now I've opened up my heart,
I say we really love you,
The two parts of my heart.

I Shed a Tear

As the waiter comes toward me,
I think of long ago,
And then I drown my sorrow,
For I still love him so.

He's on the town with someone new,
He's out, I know not where,
And here I sit, alone again,
In agonized despair.

He made me feel a tremor,
Within my guarded heart,
But now he has somebody new,
And torn it all apart.

He'll never know the way I feel,
He took no time to see,
And now that he has drifted,
Our love will never be.

I thought of him when he was here,
And even though he's gone,
I want him back each evening,
To be near him every dawn.

I fear to wake each morning,
To find he isn't near,
And surely every dawning,
I, trembling, shed a tear.

He never said he loved me,
I guess I should have known,
Loving him was foolish,
His heart is cold as stone.

I sit here now and wonder,
As I drown within my beer,
Will I ever love again?
Then I shed another tear.

In Touch Out Of Time

I came in touch with reality,
To make love to a fantasy,
Never to find tranquility,
In the realm of iniquity.

Seclusion

Though forced into seclusion,
By mishap or delusion,
Alone and panting,
Raving and ranting,
Craving a little intrusion.

The Unknown Lady.

There's a barroom in this city
Where the unknown lady goes,
And the tears that she is shedding,
Are for someone no one knows.

I stood there not so long ago,
And watched her as she danced,
I wonder if the day will come,
When she'll give me a chance.

Somewhere deep inside of her,
A lonely lady lives,
Hoping for the safe return,
Of the love she often gives.

They can't control their passion,
When ever she is near,
They overlook the tenderness,
The lady holds so dear.

If you ever get to meet her,
This unknown lady fair,
Show her that you love her,
And let us know you care.

Solitary Thought

Sitting in my solitude,
I hear you call my name.
The sound is soft and gentle,
And fresh as summer rain.

I see your smiling face,
That twinkle in your eye,
I feel your warm embrace
And trembling, hear you sigh.

Could it be your tender love
Which makes me feel this way?
Well if it is, I hope it lasts
Forever and a day.

Last Request

Weep not for me, now I am gone,
For now, I sing a different song.
My soul is where the sparrow flies,
Let not the tears come to your eyes.

Rejoice with me that I am done,
At last, my earthly race is won,
I love you more, now I am free,
I'll love you through eternity.

So grant me this, my last request,
Mourn me not upon my death,
In everlasting Peace I wait,
Until we meet at Heaven's gate.

Rings of Love

I thought that I would let you know,
How much I truly love you so.
My gift is there within your ring,
My life, my love, my everything.

The partnership these rings suggest,
Is all filled up with all the best,
The best of love I offer you,
The kind of love that's strong and true.

Although these words may simple, be,
That's how I think of you and me,
A simple love, that's simply grand
And held within a simple band.

Movement Motion

If I move you,
Like you move me
And we haven't moved all week,
Should I move for the potion
To start movement motion,
Or will you make the movement for me?

Constipation Proclamation

If chocolate flavoured X-lax,
Is what your system needs,
Why grunt and groan
Pant and moan
Until your ass hole bleeds.

Just get this famous laxative,
From your local pharmacy,
Then pass that grief
And get relief,
But please don't shit on me!

No Word - No Sound

I love you so that I could die,
But please don't ever ask me why.
That question I have pondered too,
It's all you say, and all you do.

If I would try to pin it down,
To just one word or just one sound,
The task is very hard you see,
For no word or sound says you and me.

Hard To Say

Sometimes it is so difficult,
To say what's on your mind,
You want to say it perfectly
But the words are hard to find.

All the things that need be said,
Are spoken with your eyes,
And given greater meaning
With punctuating sighs.

My Valentine 1

You're my sweetheart and my love,
You're my sunshine from above,
And the love we share together is divine.
So on this Sweetheart's Day
With sincerity I pray
That you'll consent to be my Valentine.

My Valentine 2

You're my love, you're my life,
You're my lover, you're my wife
And hand in hand, we'll pass our earthly time,
With all my heart and soul,
It's my one and only goal,
That each year you say you'll be my Valentine.

My Melody

There's nothing now, in my life,
That matters any more,
Since that night, I watched you,
Go walking out my door.

Please say that you'll forgive me,
Bring back to me my song,
I cannot live without you,
My melody is gone.

Come back to me my darling,
I'll try to make things right,
I cannot live another day
Without my morning light.

How can I say I'm sorry?
When you're so far away,
How can my heart stop aching?
When it breaks more every day.

I didn't mean to hurt you,
Didn't want to make you cry,
How could I be so foolish?
As to let you say goodbye.

Please say that you'll forgive me,
Bring back to me my song,
I cannot live without you,
My melody is gone.

Silent Partners

Deep within your silence,
Waits Anger's smoky rage,
Building the inferno
'til hatred comes of age.

No turning back the tempest,
That waits to be set free,
Smoldering in silence
It's waiting there for me

I dare not break the silence,
I dare not get too close,
I fear the slightest whisper
Would vent this rage morose.

I'll wait in painful dread,
With trembling in my stance,
Waiting for the time to come
When I'll see the fire's dance.

I'll wait in silence, hoping
That when this tempest breaks
Our love still shines behind the clouds
And pray for both our sakes.

Night Fliers

They fly on wings of gossamer
Through the silent velvety night,
Their song is high and musical
When they come near in flight.

These tiny creatures, made by God,
From watery nurseries born
Are often heard on summer nights
And sought for in the morn.

With tiny bellies bloated full
We know they've had a feast
For we, the banquet, start to itch
To kill the mosquito beast.

Patience Reward

The first time that I saw your face
You wouldn't look my way,
Men were vying for your time
So I just turned away.

I felt a warmth rise up in me
My mouth, it did go dry,
When you finally spoke to me
I thought I'd surely die.

For months, I longed to hold you close,
My dreams were filled with you,
I spent each waking moment
In hopes, they would come true.

It seemed, each time I tried to speak,
The words I planned to say,
Would somehow get all jumbled up
Then you'd shake your head and say,

Please go away, don't bother me,
Leave me alone, just let me be,
You're much too young for one like me,
Just go away, please let me be.

I tried to find another girl,
But each time that I would,
I'd speak your name instead of hers,
You know that was no good.

I thought I'd give it one more try,
To show my love inside,
I'd have to make you understand
Without you I would die.

You said that maybe you could find
Some time to make a date,
I didn't think I'd heard you right,
So I gave myself a shake.

I was the perfect gentleman,
And you, the perfect prize,
Then I felt you warm to me
As I looked into your eyes.

Now we are one, for many years,
Our vows still like a song,
The words that we cannot forget
The melody so strong.

When e'er we talk of how it was,
You smile at me that way,
I start to melt within my heart,
Then you shake your head and say,

Don't go away, it bothers me,
To be alone, don't let me be.
You're young enough for loving me,
Don't go away, you're part of me.

*P*ain

No hurt can greater be than that,
Caused by words, in anger, spat.
No greater pain the heart can stand,
Than horrors flung by words of man.

What bitter price our tempers take,
What payment, then, the heart must make.
Bitter words the tongue has hurled,
Can shake apart a lover's world.

Lovers Plea

Without your music, there is no song,
Without your words, the beauty's gone.
Without you ever by my side,
My loneliness I could never hide.

Please don't ever say we're through,
For I am not, if not for you,
You are my lover and my friend,
You are my passion to the end.

Take the fear from in my heart,
Say that we will never part,
Let me hold your love in me,
Let our love forever be.

Bitchery

Oh the bitchery of treachery
And the witchery of lechery
Oh, the wicked ways that lovers do beseech,
While the letches bitch of witchery
And the witches bitch of lechery
Neither of the lovers will they reach.

You Are

You're my life, you're my love,
You're my sunshine from above,
You're everything to me that means so much.
For the love that you are giving,
I'm so glad that we are living,
With our hearts so seldom ever out of touch.

For the love that we are sharing,
All the years of tender caring,
And the joys that loving you has given me,
You're the ruler of the part,
That is known to be my heart,
And that's the way, I know, 'twill always be.

Dance

When the music's right
And the body is willing
Give up your mind
To the dance so thrilling.

When it comes down to
The final rehearsal
You'll know that the feeling
Is universal.

Joy. Love
Freedom's expression.
The body's cure
For the mind's depression.

Dance. Dance
Dance the emotion
Dance. Dance,
Perpetual motion
Dance.

Dance to the beat
Of your body's drummer
Let all your cares
Fade into slumber.

Everyone feels
The joy you are showing
Everyone's dancing
Without even knowing.

Dance. Dance
Dance the emotion
Dance. Dance,
Perpetual motion

Joy. Love
Freedom's expression.
The body's cure
For the mind's depression.
Dance

Engagement Verse

We see that now your heart's been won,
From now, your hearts will beat as one.
The birds will sing sweet love's refrain,
As you ever walk down lover's lane.

As now you vow to each be true,
No longer will you think of You,
For now, it's We and Us and Ours.
The sun, the stars, the springtime flowers.

We wish you love along the way,
As you head toward your wedding day.
When all God's universe will sing
Of the joy that's held within your rings.

Farewell

When we are born, we're given time,
How much, we do not know,
And so we live as best we can
Until it's time to go.

But when that time is shortened
By the evil hand of Hate,
How can we tell you of our dreams?
When time just wouldn't wait.

The sorrow felt within our hearts
Long will burn within,
For now your life, untimely gone
By man's most horrid crime.

We know that you will find your peace
As we must try to do,
We know God has a special place
For one as loved as you.

Mother

I cannot seem to find the words
The words that should be said,
About the loving memories
Stored in my heart and head.

The times when I was very small
Unsure of city life,
Scared to death of crowds and cars,
You eased my childish strife.

You taught me all the little things,
That makes a person strong,
You showed me how to be myself,
Turn tragedy to song.

Though I seemed to turn my back,
On all you tried to do,
Through the trials and misery
Your love came shining through.

You gave the gift of common sense,
Of values I now hold,
And though I didn't see it then,
Your heart is solid gold.

You're Just An Angel to Me

You're just an angel to me,
Your eyes are warm as they can be,
Your skin, so soft, so heavenly,
You're just an angel to me.

When I brought you to this world
Just another baby girl,
'til 'round my heart, your fingers curled
Now you are my entire world.

When I chance to look at you,
There's nothing more that I can do,
Except to love you through and through
What more can any mother do?

You're just an angel to me,
I will love you endlessly,
Now I look at you and see,
You're just an angel to me.

Fallen Drummer

Every time you look at me,
Your eyes, a story tell,
Of the drummer in your heart,
And how that drummer fell.

The words of love you cannot speak,
Are said each time we touch,
The only words that need be said,
"I love you very much."

You say you fell when first we met,
Your heart did skip a beat,
I didn't know you'd placed your world,
There, before my feet.

Persistently, with tact and skill,
You lead the merry chase,
Though spurned, you faltered not your course,
'til now, I feel your grace.

Wedding Vow

"With this ring, I thee wed"
Are all the words that need be said,
Rings of love that have no end
Perfect lovers, perfect friends.

The symbol that each ring imparts,
The joining of two happy hearts,
The bells that ring, proclaim the joy,
That brings together girl and boy.

From this day you'll ever be,
Joined in love eternally,
Hand in hand, you'll share this life,
Ever happy, man and wife.

Baby Shower Thanks

Thank you for your gift so fine,
Mother and child are just divine,
I would say more, but what the heck,
Hope you are well, 'because Pa's a wreck.

Will I Be Heard?

I am but a molecule
In life's eternal sea,
In all of God's creation,
Too small am I to see.

If I should breach the surface,
And silent, speak my mind,
Will I make a tiny ripple,
To be felt by all mankind?

Will my thoughts go by unnoticed?
When my pen is ever stilled,
Or will God see it fitting
That my words, some hearts, have filled?

For Your Wedding

We heard you speak your tender vows,
Of love that's never ending,
The promise for a happy life,
Together you'll be spending.

Now hand in hand throughout your lives,
You'll never be alone,
In love and honor, years from now,
You'll see how much you've grown.

You share in all life has to give,
Through happiness and strife,
And grow within the love of God,
Ever happy, man and wife.

Congratulations

Congratulations, it's a boy,
May he always bring you joy,
Now it's up each morn at three,
To feed your son upon your knee

The screams and squalls that you will hear,
Will always seem too very near.
With bleary eyes, and soaking lap,
You'll be fixing drips and leaking taps.

But after all is said and done
You'll find such pride in your new son.

Sister, Dear Sister

Sister, dear sister, now what have you done,
You've taken to stealing, without any gun,
You're weapon is lies, your method discreet,
You steal from your mother through her balance sheet.

You took her possessions when she couldn't sign,
You sold off a thousand, for only a dime.
In the best of her interest, you said it was done,
But WE know you cheated, WE know what you've done.

You cried when you thought that you lost all she had
You called me to tell me so I would be sad,
You forget that I know you, the person you are,
I just never thought that you'd go this far.

How could you think that I wouldn't get wise?
That I would believe all your treacherous lies.
The evil inside you is there in your face,
No surgeon on earth could mask your disgrace.

You bewitched and beguiled all those you could use,
But in the end it is you who will lose.
You've always had everything placed in your hand,
You've never encountered the hardship of man.

You think that you've earned it, the right to it all,
But darling, dear sister, at Judgment you'll fall.
You heart is conniving and cold as a stone,
Chilled through the years by ices unknown.

A snake is to venom, as you are to deed,
Your thoughts and your actions are governed by greed.
Although I can't stop you, God knows what is best,
So you'll have your verdict when they lay you to rest.

Memories

Memories, of you,
Always on my mind,
Memories of a time,
When you loved me.

Dim lit, doorways,
Shelter from the rain,
Remembered once again
Makes me lonely.

Candles, burning,
Reflected in your eyes,
'till the morning skies
Found us loving.

Memories, of you,
Always on my mind,
Memories of a time,
When you loved me.

Tender, moments,
Holding hands with you,
Things that lovers do
When they are happy.

Golden, moments,
Laughing in the sun,
Telling everyone,
That you love me.

Memories, of you,
Always on my mind,
Memories of a time,
When you loved me.

Holding, closely,
To the words you said,
Laying in my bed
Softly weeping.

Teardrops, falling,
Rivers down my face,'
Bringing to this place,
Their silent thunder.

Memories, of you,
Always bring a tear,
Only I can hear
Their silent thunder.

Winter Comes

We know that winter always comes,
No matter how we try
To stop the snow from coming down,
So the flowers will not die.

All the things we hold so dear,
Too soon, they pass away.
Leaving only memories,
Of brighter summer days.

The cold of winter strikes the heart,
With white hot spears of pain,
We seldom see Death's dusty bloom,
When the eyes are filled with pain.

But then the seasons turn once more,
The sun will shine again,
Memories come to make us smile,
And ease the winters pain.

Though on Life's path
(She'll) He'll no more trod,
(She) He walks in Peace,
By the hand of God.

Golfers Toast

May your fairways be straight,
Hazards be few and small,
But what ever you do,
Keep your eye on the ball.

Daughter Dear Daughter

Daughter, dear daughter, now where have you gone?
I've waited since midnight, now it's nearly dawn,
You left in a hurry, I couldn't say "No',
Now daughter, dear daughter, where did you go?

Papa, dear papa, now please go to bed,
I've just gone to town for my Jimmy to wed,
He's given me diamonds; he's given me pearls,
Now I'll have his baby, we hope it's a girl.

Daughter, dear daughter, your mother's upset,
You know that she thinks you're her baby yet.
Now who is this Jimmy, and where is he from,
If he's but a rounder, I'll fetch out my gun.

Papa, dear papa, now please do not scold,
I'm no longer a baby; I'm thirty years old,
Jimmy is handsome, he's rich and he's kind,
I couldn't have got me a much better find.

Daughter, dear daughter, we wish you the best,
You know that we both pray for your happiness,
Why don't you and Jimmy stay here for a spell?
I'm sure we can all spend his money quite well.

Southampton, Ontario

Sunset on lake Huron,
A lovely site to see,
Fills the soul with gladness,
The heart, with ecstasy.

Come rest your weary body,
Gaze upon God's handicraft,
In the playground of the angels,
Where peace, the breezes waft.

A tiny town, Southampton,
Nestled on this peaceful shore,
Steeped in ancient memory,
Of peace and love and war.

Hellos from every stranger,
A smile on every face,
The town, the folk, the sunset,
With God, all dwell in grace.

Let us take our leave now,
Of this smoky, grimy town,
To settle in Southampton,
Where naught can bring us down.

Alone

She sits alone and wonders,
As she contemplates her nails,
Why homes for the elderly,
Seem so much like jails.

They tell her when to wake up,
They tell her when to sleep,
But they never tell the answers,
To the secrets that they keep.

Family comes by, now and then,
She can't remember why,
As she stares out of the window,
At the dull deserted sky.

Strange and mournful whisperings,
Go softly through her head,
Sounds of haunted laughter,
Quotes from books she's read.

She often finds him with her,
Though they tell her, he is gone,
Her husband, friend and lover,
With whom she lived so long.

In the night, when all is quiet,
He comes to ease her fears,
He tells her how he misses her,
She smiles through lonely tears.

She needs someone to lean on,
To help her in her plight,
He reaches out to hold her,
She tries to hold him tight.

Tears streaming down her face,
She screams in silent dread,
Then lays her weary body down,
On the cold and lonely bed.

"Father why'd you leave me,
When you know I need you so,
How come you didn't take me too,
When you felt it time to go"?

Merle

Merle, dear Merle,
A pearl of a girl,
Who just doesn't know when to quit,
Poor sweet Buck,
Is just out of luck,
When Merle comes to drink for a bit.

Infectious laugh,
Quite the gaff,
When you sit down to join for a spell,
Stories imparted,
Once she gets started,
Make you feel that you know her quite well.

Perky and small
A wink for us all,
Her stories seem never to end,
Talking to Merle,
This pearl of a girl,
Leaves you feeling you've just made a friend.

Winds of Spring (in Southampton)

Gentle as an angels wing,
Soft as silken veil,
Rising to a viper's fang.
Mere words could only fail.

They cut, they slice, they bite and rend,
They caress and soothe the soul,
Wrap us in a lover's balm,
Or pierce with chill untold.

The trill of laughter floating,
On wings of pure enchantment,
Or howl with the ferocity,
That only Hell can send.

The winds that through Southampton blow,
Are all and more as you well know,
But nowhere else can they be beat,
Southampton's winds blow ever sweet.

Chrystal Princess

Listen to the whisperings,
Of stories often told,
As they tumble sweetly trilling,
Over pebbles, rocks, and shoals.

Sunlight's laughter in the eyes,
Of every rushing stream,
Living, loving laughter,
Of some enchanted dream.

In all the minds imaginings,
Could nothing else come near,
To the pure and simple murmurings,
That by a brook we hear.

Rest your mind a moment,
And listen to the song,
Of the merry Chrystal Princess,
That's loved this land so long.

Her stories creep into you heart,
To fill you with delight,
Leaving, with you, a part of her,
As she takes her merry flight.

Never Parted

No one knows how many times,
I've been with you, in my mind,
No one knows how much I cared,
No one knows the love we shared.

You know I can't be with you now,
I'll get to you someday, somehow,
No one on earth will ever know,
Just how much I loved you so.

We loved the strongest near the end,
Our time apart, I can't defend.
Now we are close, though none can see,
I'm part of you, you're part of me.

When once again we've chance to talk,
Through eternity we'll walk,
But until then, I must be brave,
'til I lay with you, beside your grave.

Defiance

Let them kick while I'm down,
Let them stare at me and frown
Let them do to me whatever they can do,
For inside of me I'm strong,
And no matter what goes wrong,
They'd better watch their step, I'm coming through.

Man of Passion

Years of toil and pain and passion,
Shaped a man in his own fashion,
Scholar wise with brave ideals,
Sculptor, artist, one who heals.

Sleepless nights to make amends,
Tending close the rules he bends,
Remake, reshape that which ails,
What he attempts, never fails.

Gifted man of heart and hand,
He'll do for others, what he can,
Payment waived in time of need,
More like him, we surely need.

I knew him when, in school he be,
His children sat upon my knee,
I stand in awe, as I did then,
Of Dr. Lloyd Niels Carlsen.

Torment Eased

Empty chalice, hollow urn,
No flame of life within me burns,
Place of birth, an empty tomb,
No life to give, this barren womb.

Sacred temple, hallowed urn,
When once the flame began to burn,
Too soon it flickered out and died,
Devastated tears I cried.

How tempting 'twas to curse the Fates,
Childless life to contemplate,
No greater torment can there be,
This painful yearning deep in me.

Sinking deep into despair,
Told myself I didn't care,
Bitter woman, cold as stone,
Wretched soul all alone.

As Fate would have it, so She turned,
Filled the chalice She had spurned,
Gave to me a homeless waif,
To take my heart, and keep it safe.

Parting Thought

If tears could wash away the hurt,
Then I would gladly cry,
If it would make it easier,
For me to say goodbye.

Now as I think of what has passed,
As our time comes to and end,
It hurts me most to realize,
I leave my dearest friend.

I hope that when you think of me,
A smile comes to your face,
As I will often think of you,
In my heart you hold a place.

Leaf Like Me

I saw a leaf the other day,
Upon a tree, in gentle sway,
As it fluttered from the tree,
It seemed that leaf was just like me.

It sailed upon the gentle breeze,
To my heart, it gave a squeeze,
As I watched it floating down,
To settle lost, upon the ground.

Oh, fickle breeze did play a game,
Up it went, then down it came,
'til last it caught upon the stream,
To spin and drift, as in a dream.

Chrystal Council

Soft and gentle murmurings,
Can ease a troubled soul,
As the brook goes swiftly on its way
To its appointed goal.

Serenity pervades the scene,
The crickets sing their song,
Helping me to understand
Where my heart went wrong.

Birds are calling from on high,
They cannot feel my strife,
As by the crystal councilor,
I re-evaluate my life.

Water rushing, clear and cool,
Quench the soul that's parched,
Quietly it cools the flame,
Of anger on the march.

I try, at last, to come to terms,
With why I caused you pain,
I realize I've been a fool,
Then scan the brook again.

Darling Won't You

Darling won't you touch me?
Like you did before.
Walk with me along my lonely road.
Darling won't you love me?
Like you did before.
Kiss me with the love you always showed.

Darling won't you whisper?
Like you did before.
Murmur sweet love sayings in my ear.
Darling won't you tell me,
Like you did before?
All the things you know I long to hear.

I know you'll never touch me
Like you did before.
That is something I cannot pretend.
I never thought I'd mourn you,
Though not so any more,
Why do loved ones lives come to an end?